Earth is not the vehicle we are riding on,

we all are, an essential part of it.

Texts & Photographs by: Tilly RR

Part One: Random Thoughts & Photographs

Part Two: Splendid Spirit of Nature

Part Three: Nature's Beauty

Preface

The original concept for this project, was to put together a book of thoughts that would be uplifting and enriching to the reader, by bringing out a positive outlook on life using nature as inspiration. This collection of thoughts, is the result of unexpected moments, when words have sprouted with the urge of taking root, and flourished while being written down.

A more visual direction took effect, when I realized that I could pair some of the thoughts with nature photographs I've taken through the years. Thus, Random Thoughts and the Wisdom of Nature commenced.

It is a natural wish for any writer/photographer, whether amateur or professional, to be able to incite some kind of emotion or forward thought in his or her audience; in my case, of a positive spirit. This is my first attempt at bringing to you some enjoyment and stimulus with the beauty of nature to help me out.

Note of interest: most of the photographs in this book were taken right in my own backyard, and many of the flowers and plants shown here, have been planted by me from seed. It is very rewarding and exciting seeing them grow day by day.

If only for one moment: a smile came to your face, a happy memory was remembered, amazement was once felt again, a realization is grasped, a new appreciation is attained, or a simple peaceful moment enjoyed, then, the wish has been fulfilled.

Putting this book together, is but the beginning of a long learning process. Discovering all the beauty that surrounds us and that we forget to appreciate at times, can awaken some wonderful things in everyone.

It is amazing how we can still hold some amount of individuality in a world of mass herding, created by ourselves. Explore yours!

Gladiolus

African Iris

Random Thoughts & Photographs

It may be debatable, whether this part of the book should have been called, Random Photographs & Thoughts. At the end, I figured it is a personal opinion, so you decide.

Diligently, I tried to find good partners between the words and the pictures, in which the feeling of the thought and the essence of the photo, could unite to create a pleasant moment for the reader.

You will not find any particular order followed in these coming pages, however, some care was taken in achieving some coherence.

Canna Lily

Why do we like photographs; is it
because we can relive a moment in time, or
perhaps discover another angle on life?

Cossandra
Orange Marmalade

A bloom a day, can keep your gloom away.

Bee & Wildflower

In order to live in balance, you must
try to understand the cycles of life.

Green Anole Lizard

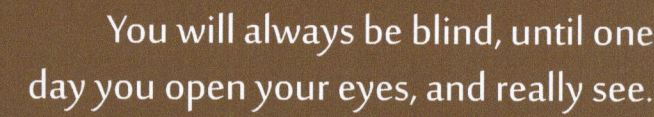

You will always be blind, until one
day you open your eyes, and really see.

Red Cabbage

It is really quite simple...
once you peel beyond its complexity.

Bells of Ireland

With patience, love and nourishment,
you can grow just about anything.

Papaya Flower

Nature nourishes more than our physical being,
it is essential to sustaining our spiritual well-being.

Royal Water Lily

When you look into a pond,
and see your reflection... smile.

Muscovy Duck

Think about what really makes you
happy or brings you joy, and just do it.

Parrot Tulips

Live a colorful life.

Lady Pig
in a bed of Kung Pao hot peppers

No matter the situation,
let your light shine through.

Daisy Bud

If you are sad and lonely,
look for something beautiful in nature
and spend some time with it.

Spinyback Orbweaver

Even that at times, life is a tangle of webs,
you may still find some beauty entangled within.
If that fails, imagination can be boundless.

Coleus

Splendid Spirit of Nature

In this section, I want to share with you some of the beauty that surrounds us. From the more majestic vistas and natural wonders, to the smallest details on a simple flower or animal.

Never stop looking around you and always keep in touch with nature. The splendid spirit of nature is there for you to discover and marvel at. Care for it.

I've included a few tidbits on each photo's subject, which I thought could be interesting and fun to learn about.

Desert Rose

Not a rose but a succulent, it likes hot & sunny conditions.
Interesting how the flower is so "icy" in color. The milky sap
is poisonous, and used in Africa to make poison arrows.

Festive Marigold

"Day of the Dead" Mexican celebration's official flower.
Their aroma & colors are said to attract the dead's spirit,
allowing it to celebrate the joy of the life they once had.

Colorful Water Lilies

The Lotus, as known by ancient Egyptians, is greatly connected with their culture. Some flowers open in the morning and close & sink under water at night, others the reverse. It was used as a motif associated with their beliefs on death and the afterlife.

Pleasanton, California

Even though it is considered part of the San Francisco Bay area, this city has spaces that still remind you of how it used to be when population was less & a simpler life was lived.

Grotto Geyser, Yellowstone

Grotto is the namesake for this group of fountain-type geyser.
The pool from which it erupts, is hidden inside these unique
sediment formations, which are created by the sediment
as it coats old tree stumps, that stand nearby the pool.

Thermals, Yellowstone

The bacteria on these thermals is called cyanobacteria and it can live in temperatures as hot as 167° F. Where the water is hottest, the color is more yellow and green, and where it is cooler the water changes towards orange and rust hues.

Taro Leaf

Commonly known as elephant ears because of the shape of the leaves, which can reach 3 feet in size. The taro root is edible if cooked, similar to a potato. Even though this leaf is past its time, it still shows us there is beauty in everything, when you take the time to look close enough.

Copperleaf Plant

The different shades and shapes in the Copperleaf plant
are a delight to the eyes, from its leaves to its flowers.
Though a native of Fiji and nearby islands, it is
very common in South Florida.

Cinnabar Mushroom

Its favorite food is cherry wood, but oak is okay too. Belongs to the polypore group, which has many edible mushrooms and no poisonous ones. However, the Cinnabar is too tough to eat, but very striking to the eye. It could even be pictured inside a marine aquarium.

Leucocoprinus Mushrooms

Poisonous only if eaten. Common in flower pots and very hard to get rid of, so it's best to learn to love them. Luckily, they are charmingly pretty. The "Flowerpot Parasol" is not harmful to other plants.

Condy Anemone

Found mainly in waters near Florida, these anemones live in loose groups instead of colonies and can have a lifespan of over 10 years. The pink tips, look like neon lights.

Zoanthid Coral

Soft colonial corals, that typically spread in a 360° pattern. They are made up of many circular polyps, which look like small individual anemones. They are shunned by most predators, due to their potently poisoned tissue.

Shy Dragonfly

Ancient insects, the largest dragonfly fossil had a wingspan of
nearly 3 feet. They have 2 pairs of wings, which allow them
to move in any direction and even hover in place.
They are also very fast and can reach 30 mph.

Pumpkin Flower

Both female & male flowers are present in the same vine. All parts of the plant are edible, including its bright flowers. These are shortlived, so catch them quickly and try them.

Hibiscus Flower

Not only a beautiful flower. All parts of the Hibiscus plant are very useful; from food to fiber; from medicine to shampoo. The red calyces are widely used as food coloring.

Vanda Orchid

With their innocent color and exotic shape, the pink orchid stands for pure affection for the one you love. Vanda orchids are given to commemorate the 14th wedding anniversary.

Bird of Paradise

This native of South Africa, has long inspired artists with its exotic and unusual beauty. Symbolisms such as freedom and joy, have also been attributed to this exquisite flower.

Red Daisy

The word daisy means day's eye. The daisy is really a mix of 2 flowers; the ray floret or outer petals, and the disk floret, the center. The leaves are edible, used in salads.

Bengal Canna Lily

The most beautiful of the Cannas, it is related to the banana tree and can be grown as an aquatic plant also. The Victorians were fascinated by the drama it could bring to their gardens.

Ginger Flower

The flower conjures images of the exotic. Ginger has been cultivated for so long, its origin is not clear. The root has been used as an herb for its pungent flavor, and also in medicinal and aromatic therapies, as a tonic and stimulant for many ailments.

Knight Anole
*After eating a
mango from my tree*

Nature's Beauty

I feel fortunate to have been able to capture the photos you'll see in the next pages. It is truly a treasure to have such a diverse natural world, right here, all around us. We spend too much time inside 4 walls, whether physical or figurative; and not enough absorbing the gifts given freely to us by nature.

There are so many places still to discover and I hope I will be able to see some of them before I'm too old to travel.

But remember, that even in your own backyard or neighborhood, there is always something to marvel at... if you look ...and really see.

Whidbey Island
Washington State

This is Coupeville, a quaint town in Whidbey Island, off the coast of Washington State. Though only 25 miles from Seattle, this small island pleasantly moves at a different rythm than the nearby cities on the mainland. Everywhere you look, you can find amazing vistas, unspoiled by civilization. The food is homegrown and delicious and several vineyards can be explored at leasure. Very relaxing.

White Peacock Butterfly

This is a common butterfly in Florida. They love my Basil flowers. I never get tired of watching them; they make me think of a stainglass on an art canvas.

Boone
North Carolina

Morning mist amongst the mountains, during a beautiful Autum day in North Carolina. If you have never experienced this season, make time to do so. The hues of oranges, yellows, reds and greens you'll see everywhere you look, will warm your heart and soul.

Very peculiar the flower of the Tomatillo, when seen up-close. You don't expect to find such rich textures and colors in this tiny flower. Later, a husk-like cocoon forms and encases the tangy green berry while it grows. It is pretty cool to see its development.

Tomatillo Flower

Pine Bark

The different textures and the geometric designs nature has created here, are a tiny drop in all the variations we can find out there. A generous tree, its strong wood is widely used.

Calla Lily

The beauty of this lily,
lies in its simplicity.
There aren't many petals
or other elements to its
construction, which you
find in many flowers,
however, it provokes
thoughts of purity.

Champery
Switzerland

The magical beauty of this place is breathtaking. Your eyes wander all around you, as if you were a child again, dreaming, and not wanting to wake-up just yet.

Columbine

What a complex looking flower.
Both beautiful when opened or
closed. The Columbines are
exquisite flowers and there are a
lot of varieties and colors. They
are bound to make you smile.

Old Church, Ireland

It is so important that we do preserve our past. It shows us where we came from, and guides us to where we are going. When you see an old building such as this, it makes you wonder all that it has seen and heard, all the lifes it has touched. It gives us a sense of existence; it grounds us.

Long ago, when photographs were not around, people still had their own picture memory galleries. Look around for the beauty in nature and really see it and feel its healing power.
Create your own picture memory gallery; no camera needed.

Sanchezia

Well readers, the end of this book is here, and I hope it will not be my last. I will like to leave you with another random thought. It is meant to make you reflect within yourself, and hopefuly, set you off on a new journey of self discovery.

ANOTHER THEORY OF RELATIVITY

Everything is relative to you and yours.

Today, you climbed a mountain...
...you finally signed up for the dancing
lessons you've always wanted to take.
This is your Everest.

Today, you forgave someone...
...you forgave yourself.
This is your act of kindness.

Today, you sailed an ocean...
...you lost a loved one.
This is one journey you have endured.

Today, you make a discovery...
...you wake up and it's a beautiful day.
This is your life, relative to you and your loved ones.
Turn your theory of relativity, into your truth.

Mandevilla

Share your thoughts after reading
my book, I will love to hear them.
Write to me at: trr810@yahoo.com

www.ingramcontent.com/pod-product-compliance
Lightning Source LLC
Chambersburg PA
CBHW050833290526
45792CB00001B/379